GEORGE WASHINGTON WILSON

in

DUNDEE & ANGUS

Acknowledgements

Many people have given generously of their time to help me in the preparation of this book. Much of the preliminary footwork was done by Mrs Heather Lyall while working as a research assistant, and I am particularly grateful to Mr Thomas Haining, C.M.G., Research Fellow of the University of Aberdeen, who took so much time and pains to research the history of Brechin where he has settled. It has proved extremely difficult to prune so much good information to meet the demands of this type of publication. Miss Jennifer Ingram, Research Assistant in the Department of Geography at St Andrews, brought a historical geographer's perspective to our travels around the various localities featured. It was good of her to participate so helpfully and enthusiastically. Dr Colin MacLachlan, a Dundonian himself (though not quite venerable enough to recall life pre-1914), checked the Dundee section.

As ever, Mike Craig and Caroline Gilbert of the Photographic Unit, Aberdeen University Library were helpfulness itself in preparing prints, and Mary Murray's assistance was invaluable. The cost of much of the travel was met by a grant from the University of Aberdeen Development Trust. Norma Sim, Secretary of the Department of Economic History, typed the text speedily and accurately. My wife, under duress, brought her critical eye to bear on spelling, punctuation and language. To all of these I offer my thanks.

Bibliography

The Ordnance *Gazetteer of Scotland* (various editions) is an invaluable source, as are the various guides to Scotland such as Murray's *Handbook* and Baddeley's *Through Guide*. Slater's *Directory* contains much local information and the Railway Companies issued promotional material such as *Through Scotland by the Caledonian Railway* or *The Beauties of Scotland* (The North British Railway Official Guide).

For the particular localities, Dundee is best-covered with Charles McKean and David Walker's splendid *Dundee: An illustrated Introduction* (1984). There is also Peter Adamson and R. Lamont-Brown, *Victorian and Edwardian Dundee and Broughty Ferry from old photographs* (1984).

A fine contemporary source is David Barrie, *The City of Dundee Illustrated* (1890). For Arbroath see G. Hay, *Arbroath* (1899); for Montrose, either G. Walker, *Guide to Montrose* (1988) or D. P. Davidson, *Tourist's Guide to Montrose* (n.d., c.1889). Forfar's history is well served by Alan Reid, *The Royal Burgh of Forfar*. Kirriemuir generated a surprising number of guides, all hanging on Barrie's coat tails: J. Stirton, *Thrums and its Gems* (1896) or J. F. Mills, *Through Thrums: a handbook for visitors* (1896). Brechin and Edzell are well covered by D. H. Edwards, *Historical Guide to Brechin* (1902), and *Round the Ancient City* (c. 1900).

Published by AUL Publishing, Queen Mother Library,
Meston Walk, Aberdeen AB9 2UE (Tel. 0224 272594).

Printed in Scotland by Waverley Press (Aberdeen) Ltd.

GEORGE WASHINGTON WILSON

in

DUNDEE & ANGUS

ALASTAIR J. DURIE

Photographs from the George Washington Wilson Collection

Edited for the Library Committee of the University of Aberdeen by
Peter L. Payne

George Washington Wilson by Sir George Reid RSA
(reproduced by kind permission of Aberdeen Art Gallery & Museums)

Editor's Preface

The University of Aberdeen's collection of George Washington Wilson photographic negatives has justifiably been described as a "most valuable storehouse of topographical material." It is more than that: these negatives, which date from c. 1870 to 1908, portray many facets of the infinite variety of late Victorian and Edwardian life not only in Britain but in several places overseas. The collection, consisting of no fewer than 45,000 glass negatives, comprises what was essentially the stock in trade of George Washington Wilson & Co. when that company went into liquidation in 1908. Started in the early 'fifties by George Washington Wilson, a portrait miniaturist who quickly perceived the commercial potentialities of photography and who pioneered both new methods utilising the wet collodion process (particularly "instantaneous" photography) and remarkably efficient mass production techniques, Wilson combined an artistic sensitivity with great entrepreneurial flair. The firm he created became probably the most important commercial enterprise of its kind in the closing decades of the nineteenth century, enjoying a greater reputation and a larger sale than its principal rivals, the firms established by James Valentine, Francis Frith, William Lawrence and Francis Bedford. The University's collection has been dipped into to illustrate several important studies in economic and social history and George Washington Wilson himself and the firm that he founded has been the subject of a fascinating monograph by Roger Taylor, *George Washington Wilson: Artist and Photographer, 1823-1893* (Aberdeen University Press, 1981), but the riches of this magnificent collection remain largely unexploited. It is the object of this series of booklets to reveal the great historical and sociological value of the Wilson collection and to provide a fresh viewpoint on the life and landscape of late Victorian Britain and those parts of the world "covered" by the photographers employed by the firm.

This is the fourth contribution to the series by Alastair J. Durie whose enthusiasm for "GWW" and his photographs continues unabated. We are greatly indebted to him for, yet again, preparing the Introduction and providing such lively and provocative captions.

Peter L. Payne

Introduction

Angus has long had its enthusiasts: "Everything dear to tourist, antiquary and artist held in ample measure within the compactly comprehensive bounds of Forfarshire. Historic, Romantic, and Picturesque it need fear no rival" (David Reid, *Picturesque Forfarshire,* 1904). Yet for all its attractions it was a part of Scotland surprisingly neglected by George Washington Wilson, Victorian Scotland's foremost photographer. Born in 1823, the second son of a soldier turned Banffshire crofter, Wilson had started his professional career as a portrait painter, but had quickly diversified into the new art of photography. Based in Aberdeen, by the 1870s he had built up one of the largest and most prosperous photographic businesses in Britain, with thousands of topographic views available in all parts of the country. That being said, the firm's 1877 catalogue could list only six views for Forfarshire, all of Arbroath Abbey. The series of tourist booklets—some twenty of so—brought out in the same decade by the firm at a price of 1/- (5p) each, covered all the major towns in Scotland except Dundee, a number of leading resorts—Dunkeld, Elgin and Nairn— and several picturesque localities—Glencoe, Loch Lomond and Killiecrankie—but not a Forfarshire scene was featured. There was little change by 1893 when GWW died; the firm's catalogue of stereoscopic views was still very limited with only six views added, all of the Old Tay Bridge, immediately before and after the accident of 1879. Thereafter, however, the firm's holdings of Forfarshire were dramatically to expand. The 1903 catalogue listed 299 views and lantern slides available; 39 of Dundee, very nearly as many of Brechin, and over twenty of several other places in the county.

Why was there such a drive in the 1890s to cover Angus, and why had Wilson, the doyen of Scottish photographers, so signally failed to deal with the area during his lifetime? He and his assistant, William Gellie, did visit Arbroath Abbey in the late 1860s (plates 38 to 40) but otherwise nothing much appears to have captured his attention, even if three Dundee pictures (plates 13, 16a and 16b) are his. The reason for GWW's neglect lies, I think, in his market sense.

Though part of his business rested on portrait photography in his Aberdeen studio, its heart lay in the sale of scenes and views to tourists and armchair travellers. His skill in this area was recognised at the highest level of society: did not Queen Victoria herself commission GWW to illustrate with 42 photographs the special 1868 edition of *Leaves from the Journal of our Life?* The association with Victoria, recognised by his title of Photographer to Her Majesty, went back to the mid 1850s and the rebuilding of Balmoral; it was certainly an asset to an emerging photographer like Wilson. So also was his technical skill; in an interview after his father's death in 1893, A. J. Wilson stressed that although GWW had a superb natural eye for the composition of a picture, he was never anything other than painstaking in his preparation.

> "It was not only as revelations of the beauties of the Highlands but also as an account of their unique artistic merits that Mr Wilson's photographs of Scotch scenery became so popular. There was no hurry-scurry, no scamping or 'dodging' in Mr Wilson's work."
>
> ("A Pioneer in Photography, Reminiscences of the late Mr G. W. Wilson," *Aberdeen Free Press,* June 1893).

Important though royal patronage was, and however essential the artistic skill of GWW,

a third element underpinned his success. This was his business sense, his perception of where the market lay, and his ability to respond. What determined his choice of subjects was the question of whether the view would sell. That is why he paid so much attention in the 1870s to the Highlands, an area then becoming immensely popular, and why his enthusiasm remained so high for Edinburgh, then as now a tourist Mecca. And this 'bias' continued throughout his lifetime which accounts, I think, for the lack of interest in Angus which was a locality relatively late into the tourist trade. If he had been interested in people at work, Dundee's mills might have drawn him, but he was never attracted by industrial Scotland. Only fishing, a very special case, features in his work, and handloom weaving (plate 59), by the 1880s as much a curiosity as it is today, a once proud craft in decline.

Tourism in Angus had a respectable pedigree; the ruins of Arbroath Abbey had attracted visitors such as Dr Johnson (1773), Burns (1787) and Scott (1814) amongst others, but it only really took off on a large scale in the last quarter of the nineteenth century. Vital to this expansion was the railway network, which first promoted excursions within the area from the 1830s onwards and then, particularly after the completion of the second Tay Bridge, encouraged a flow of longer-distance travellers to such destinations as Edzell and elsewhere. The Caledonian Railway's handbook *Through Scotland,* commented in 1901 that "It has only been of late that the valley of the North Esk has been discovered by sightseers, the discovery having been aided by the opening of the railway to Edzell."

The boom in travel is readily traced in the local press. The *Arbroath Guide* stated in 1869 that more than half the population of the town had travelled somewhere by rail during the local holiday weekend at the end of June; 857 had gone on a special to Aberdeen, 859 to Dundee and 344 to Montrose. Sea trips went to St Andrews and the Isle of May, and the local horsehirers and their "machines" had been fully booked weeks before the holidays. Travellers meant business for hotels, lodgings, tea-rooms and ice-cream parlours, and publishers were quick to prepare the local guides. Typical of these is Davidson's *Tourist Guide to Montrose* (1884), the work of a local bookseller, which described places of interest in and around the town, and trips further afield. In "presenting to an indulgent public, the first essay towards a popular Guide Book" of Montrose, Davidson anticipated that the work would be of "great advantage to tourists and others in forming an estimate to places best adapted for spending their leisure hours" (Preface, IV). Sixteen pages of advertisements confirmed the kind of business expected from visitors. H. McArthur of the White Horse Stables offered to contract with "Pic-nic and Jaunting Parties" and Davidson himself had a circulating library for wet days, as well as £1 Tourist's Landscape or Marine Telescopes. As well as local publications, such as D. H. Edwards' *Pocket History of Brechin,* John Mills' *Through Thrums: A handbook for visitors to Kirriemuir,* there were the national guides, which were used by upper- and middle-class people to plan their holidays and whose judgements were important. It cannot have been encouraging to Arbroath to find itself curtly dismissed in the 1882 edition of A&C Black's *Picturesque Tourist of Scotland* as possessing "little to attract the tourist except its Abbey!"

What drew tourists to Angus were things like sport—especially golf—scenery

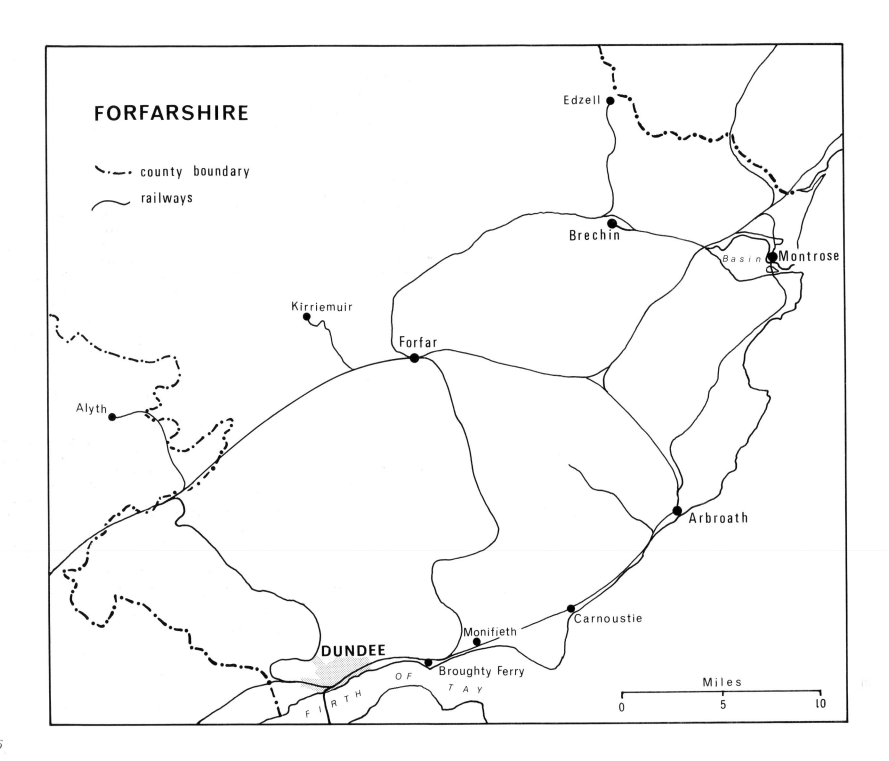

FORFARSHIRE

county boundary
railways

Edzell

Brechin

Basin Montrose

Kirriemuir

Forfar

Alyth

Arbroath

Carnoustie

Monifieth

DUNDEE

Broughty Ferry

FIRTH OF TAY

Miles

0   5   10

and history. The prospectus (c. 1900) of the enterprising manageress of the Panmure Arms Hotel in Edzell was carefully baited:

"This clean and salubrious Village is about four hours' journey from Edinburgh and Glasgow, and two hours' journey from Dundee and Aberdeen, being easily reached by rail on the Caledonian Route, and is situated in the heart of a country of great interest to tourists, and highly recommended by the medical faculty as a health resort. The air is dry and bracing, and there is no district in the East of Scotland where there are so many varied and beautiful drives. The scenery is picturesque and mountainous. Edzell Castle, now in ruins, was once the seat of the powerful family of Lindsay, Gannochy Bridge and 'The Burn', about a mile north-east of the village, are among the most romantic spots in the neighbourhood. The public roads are splendid for cycling; excellent postal arrangements; delivery of letters morning and evening. Established and United Free Churches.
This first-class Family and Tourist Hotel is fitted up with all the latest improvements and is lighted by electricity.
Salmon Fishing on the North Esk for Visitors. Excellent Billiard Table, 18-Hole Golf Course.''

Note the emphasis on the accessibility by rail, the scenery and history, the quality of the roads, and the fishing available nearby. To a modern eye the mention of the local churches and the excellent postal arrangements seem peculiarly Victorian as was the insistence on the healthiness of the area. The last was a virtue made much of by other Angus towns, though Montrose perhaps took things to an extreme; Walker's *Tourist Guide to Montrose* published in 1888 actually quoted in extenso from the annual report of the burgh's Medical Officer of Health. Dr Lawrence was confident that "for promoting health and affording enjoyment" few towns or places of resort in Britain could establish "higher claims to the public favour than Montrose."

Golf was another attraction to draw visitors to Angus. Carnoustie is an apt illustration of this, rising from insignificance in mid-century to become a favourite with many summer visitors. The Caledonian Railway went as far as to publish in its *Summer Tours Guide* (1895) a list of golf courses in Scotland which their stations serviced; Edzell (5 holes), Brechin (6), Arbroath (18), Forfar (18), Kirriemuir, Ladies and Gents (9 each), Monifieth (15), Montrose, Ladies and Gents (18 each), were the Angus representatives. Especially noticed was Carnoustie, reckoned second only to St. Andrews as a golfing resort. Golf had ceased to be an upper class preserve, thanks to the invention of the putty golf ball which made the game much less expensive for the novice or wild hitter. On the other hand, fishing and shooting—deer, grouse or pheasant—tended to remain out of reach of any other than the wealthy elite. They came north by train each August for the Twelfth, and part of the attraction of the great houses such as Kinnaird Castle (plate 74) was the shooting: duck, snipe, plovers, partridges, even capercaillie. The higher ground of the country had several good grouse moors and deer forests. Knockshannoch, for example, at the time averaged 700 grouse each season from a mere 1800 acres. Fern, near Brechin, did even better.

To the Tourer, cyclist, sportsman (or woman), swimmer or walker, Angus offered much, and its attractions were promoted fairly and successfully, with no stone left unturned. It is noticeable, for instance, how quick Kirriemuir was to exploit its favourite son, J. M. Barrie, whose early novels *Auld Licht Idylls* (1888) and *A Window in Thrums* (1889) were set there: Thrums boots and bridies, even whisky, appeared for the benefit of those who visited Kirriemuir to pay homage to the author. There was nothing new about the use of literary association—Auchmithie, as every guide pointed out, was the Mussel Crag of Scott's *Antiquary*—but the pace of Kirriemuir's publicity was a tribute to the drawing power of Barrie. And the photographers were not slow to respond either: George Washington Wilson & Co., in the person of John Hay Wilson, one of George Washington Wilson's sons, added Kirriemuir to their catalogue in the late 1890s (plates 58 to 63), perhaps with the intention of producing a parallel volume to their *Land of Scott*.

The growing popularity of Angus therefore, as a tourist area was the fundamental reason for the intense activity in the area of G. W. Wilson & Co. from the late 1880s onwards. They may well have considered staying out; after all, their only serious competitor in Scotland was based at Dundee, Valentine and Sons of 152 Perth Road (Studio: 4 High Street), and all the Angus towns had their own photographers. But they took the plunge and adopted an interesting strategy. Sometimes they sent their own photographers; Robert Beavan tackled Dundee and, as mentioned above, John Hay Wilson covered Kirriemuir. But more often than not G. W. Wilson & Co. bought in the work of local men—Frank Gillies of Broughty Ferry, John Carr at Montrose, John Geddes at Arbroath, Andrew McNair at Dundee. These photographs were then dubbed with the G. W. Wilson brandname. Only the Copyright Office Records, which required not just the name of the Proprietor of the Copyright (in this case, G. W. Wilson & Co.) but the Name and Place of Abode of the Author, can clarify who did what. And most intriguingly what also emerges is that the Aberdeen firm used photographs taken by their Dundee archrival, Valentine's, the business that was to outlast them.

It has been customary to regard the relationship of the two biggest photographic businesses in Scotland as one of straight competition. John Hannary in a article some years ago in the *British Journal of Photography* (6 August 1975) referred to this rivalry:

"Valentine's pictures surprisingly sold for more in some cases than Wilson's—Valentine's selling at 4d and 6d each while G. W. Wilson priced all of his 4d.''

But by the 1890s the situation was changing to something rather cosier. Valentine's were moving out of print selling to concentrate on the production of picture postcards, whereas Wilson & Co. were still (probably wrongly) producing prints and lantern slides. For whatever reason, the two firms began to collaborate. In *Photographs of Scottish Scenery* published by G. W. Wilson & Co. in c. 1900 there were twenty views; only two were "GWW" with all the rest (bar one) "JV." I have included the view printed of Broughty Ferry Station, "108 JV" (plate 24), to illustrate the degree of collusion.

But whatever the source, one tradition remained inviolate. The commitment to quality set by GWW himself was continued throughout the lifetime of the firm until it finally went out of business in 1907, unable to cope with the new environment of more and more people owning their own cameras (one in ten by c. 1900). The views reproduced here confirm, I hope, how high their standards were and they offer us a fascinating insight to life in Victorian Angus. Some things have changed a great deal, other facets hardly at all, but it is sobering to think of what has gone, not least the people caught in these photographs.

DUNDEE & THE TAY BRIDGE

With its rapidly increasing population and thriving textile works, late nineteenth century Dundee was regarded as the "most pushing town in Scotland" (*Caledonian Railway Through Scotland,* 1903) but guide books spent less time on it proportionately than any other large burgh in Scotland, and in truth its prosperity was not scenic, except from a distance. Large fortunes were made in the town, but not shared: it was a city of mass poverty, reflected—in the words of the Dundee historian William M. Walker (1979)—in its number of physically retarded children, overworked women and demoralised men. Yet "Juteopolis," for all that it was a manufacturing town, did have many points of attraction for the Victorian photographer. The Law, for instance, offered (and offers yet) one of the finest vantage points in the East of Scotland. And Dundee did have its share of fine buildings and streets even if all too much has succumbed to twentieth-century decay or demolition. William McGonagall's stanza catches something of the pride of Victorian Dundee folk in their city.

> There is no other town I know of which you can compare
> For spinning mills and lasses fair
> And for stately buildings there's none can excel
> The beautiful Albert Institute or the Queen's Hotel.
> "Bonnie Dundee in 1878," *More Poetic Gems*

1 The Old Tay Bridge, Summer 1879.
Looking from Fife, the first Tay Bridge (opened in May 1878) stretches the two miles across to Dundee where dozens of mill chimneys rise. In line with the end of the bridge stands the massive Cox's Stack of the Camperdown Works. The Law—without War Memorial—is clearly visible as are the Sidlaws in the distance. The North British signalman—perhaps the same Thomas Barclay who was on duty on the fateful night of 28th December 1879 when the 13 central spans of the Bridge collapsed into the river, taking with it the 4.15 from Edinburgh—leans over the guard rails at the back of his box watching GWW at work. In the right foreground (see front cover) Wilson's assistant William Gellie is beside the photographic tent, with plate boxes roundabout.

2 The New and the Old Tay Bridge

Sir Thomas Bouch's reputation collapsed along with his bridge, and W. H. Barlow's more robust design was adopted by the North British Railway Company. The contractors, William Arroll and Company, started work on the replacement bridge in June 1882. Five years later the new bridge was opened for traffic at a cost of £670,000 and thirteen lives, due in almost every case ''to the individual recklessness of the men themselves'' (Crawford Barlow, *The New Tay Bridge*, 1888) in not taking enough care on the high parts of the structure. This picture shows work on the two bridges in progress, with girders being transferred from the old to the new preparatory to the first being dismantled completely. Other materials—cylinders, new girders, ties, etc.—were constructed in Glasgow, and then floated out on pontoons from the Company workshops at the South End. While everyone knows McGonagall's poem on the original bridge, fewer are familiar with his offering to the sequel:

> ''Beautiful new railway bridge of the Silvery Tay,
> With thy beautiful side screens along your railway,
> Which will be a great protector on a windy day,
> So as the railway carriages won't be blown away,
> And ought to cheer the hearts of the passengers night and day.''
> *Poetic Gems.*

3 The New Tay Bridge

The contractor's workshops have gone and all that remains of the Old Bridge are the stumps ('cutwaters') of the piers, still to be seen today. The New Bridge opened for goods traffic on the 12th June 1887, and for passenger traffic eight days later, and it was just as well that it was wider than its predecessor, double rather than single-tracked, because within a few months over 100 trains a day were using the Bridge. Here a local from Tayport pauses at Wormit Station prior to the crossing. A lady is waiting on the opposite platform for a Dundee train to arrive. Prominent amongst the hoardings is an advertisement for the *Dundee Courier*, established in 1816 and published daily—price ½d.

TRAINING SHIP "MARS", & BRIG FRANCIS MOLISON, NEWPORT. 13570. C.NOV.

4 The Training Ship Mars

The *Mars* started life in 1848 as a two-decked 80 gun line of battle ship but was converted into a training ship in 1866, and anchored in the Tay from 1869 to provide discipline and practical education for boys in need, either orphaned or delinquent. In the summer of 1879, the *Mars* had fired a salute for Queen Victoria as her royal train crossed the Tay; six months later the *Mars* boats were out searching for survivors (there were none) of the collapse. The brig was used for sail-instruction and named after one of the city of Dundee's most generous benefactors, Francis Mollison, who had financed the construction of the Institution for the Blind at Magdalen Green. The *Mars* served not just Dundee, but elsewhere in the East of Scotland: the General Committee membership included the Lord Provost, Dean of Guild and three members of the Town Council of Edinburgh.

DUNDEE FROM LAW HILL. 19,556. C.NOV.

5 Dundee from Lawhill, c. 1890

At least thirty mill chimneys are visible in the view from the Law, the Tay and Ward works being especially prominent towards the New Tay Bridge. The *Mars* can be glimpsed against the Fife shore. Immediately below the hill lies prosperous Adelaide Place, home in 1891 to several merchants, ministers of the Free and United Presbyterian churches, and to two pawnbrokers, whose premises were in nearby Hilltown.

6 Dundee, looking south-east from the Law

The Royal Infirmary lies to the left in this picture. Built in the mid-1880s, its completion coincided with an unusually quiet time for Dundee's medical services, and it was offered to the government as a hospital for Crimean invalids. Pretty soon, however, its 220 beds were full with locals, and subsequently its accommodation was enlarged to 400. London architects were employed for the plans, and it was their unfamiliarity with the realities of Dundee's climate that led to the selection of Caenstone for the facings, all of which had to be replaced at great expense.

7 The Caledonian Railway's West Station, Dundee

This handsome station was a replacement for an earlier building. Opened in 1889 it served Perth, and via Lochee Newtyle, Coupar Angus and Blairgowrie. Cheap Saturday excursions were run to these towns and Perth at a standard charge of 1/- (5p) for the double journey, leaving just after 2 p.m. and returning in the evening. A CR horse-drawn coach waits at the front entrance. The West Station was demolished to make way for the Tay Road Bridge approaches.

8 The Esplanade, Dundee
An elegantly clad lady cyclist pauses to pose for the photographer, perhaps after calling at Dawson's Cycle and Electrical Engineering works, agents for Dunlop tyres. There are several tarpaulined wagons in the goods yard of the Tay Bridge Station and a city watercart (number 3) is refilling in the station entrance. This whole area had been reclaimed by the Railway Companies acting in concert with the Harbour Trust, a relationship which was deeply suspicious to some Dundonians such as David Barrie.

9 Tidal Basin, Royal Arch, Dundee
Telford's gates to the Earl Grey Dock, formed in 1830, are shut and not much appears to be happening on this pleasant morning, a Sunday perhaps? The crane on Observatory quay is still, and no signs of action are visible around the ship tied up in the William IV Dock. Notice the railway wagons: the harbour area was serviced by miles of railway track. The Royal Arch is visible, and to the right is the steeple of St Paul's.

10 The Royal Arch, Dundee

Ten-past-four in the afternoon, and the photographer finds himself at the Royal Arch, one of the most famous Dundee landmarks. A temporary arch had been erected in September 1844 to welcome the visit of Victoria and Albert, landing at Dundee from the royal yacht *en route* to Blair Athol. Local enthusiasm being kindled, a permanent arch was built in 1853 at a cost of over £3000 at the east end of Dock Street where it stood for over a hundred years until swept away, like the West Station, for the Tay Road Bridge. Profusely ornamented, its style was regarded by some as ''singular rather than beautiful'': what Victoria herself thought is not known. An elderly coal-wagon stands somewhat unevenly to the left, and in King William Dock are several Dundee ('DE') fishing boats.

11 The Jetty, Dundee

The sailing ship *Alcester* with magnificent figurehead is tied up at Marine Parade, along with several other ships in what had become by the late nineteenth century one of the busiest harbours in Britain. Built at Greenock in 1883 by Russell & Co for a Liverpool firm, she was 257 feet long. The iron hull could not save her, however, as Lloyds reported her wrecked in February 1897.

12 Camperdown Dock, Dundee

Over £1m was spent in the nineteenth century to improve and enlarge Dundee's port facilities, work that made it one of the finest, safest and most convenient harbours in Britain. The Camperdown docks, completed in the mid-1870s, lay further to the east. The *Falls of Dee* lies in a north-south berth by the entrance to the Victoria Docks. One of a class of ships with similar names, she was built in 1882 by Russell and Co. of Greenock and was Glasgow-owned. Unloaded here, we can only speculate that she was carrying jute, whereas the ship to the left appears to have discharged a raft of timber. Familiar present-day landmarks include the granary and the Old Steeple of St Mary's.

13 The Old Customs House, Dundee

This ancient property, no. 3., the Greenmarket, had started life in the sixteenth century as a Provost's town house, and then became the city's custom house. After the erection in 1843 of the much grander new Customs House and Harbour Chambers, it was used by various retailers. In this view, c. 1870, it houses a spirit dealer, of which Dundee had all too many, and two china firms. The turn-of-the-century occupant, James McLean, a wholesale and retail glass, china and stoneware merchant, advertised no. 3. as the "Oldest House in Dundee."

14 High Street, Dundee c. 1907

The panorama of the south side of the High Street runs from the elegant Town House of Adams (1734), with its much loved "pillars," past an eighteenth-century house in reasonable repair, to the Royal Bank buildings of 1899, whose architect G. W. Brown shared Christian names with George Washington Wilson. Another bank, the Clydesdale, is at the east end of the Square. A convoy of electric trams waits at the junction, carrying advertisements for Zebra grate polish, the Theatre and the Tabernacle, the last not a place of worship, but apparently the premises of an antique furniture dealer. In all the thronging populace, there is not a single bare head.

16a and 16b Two early views of the High Street, Dundee
Note the absence of the trams shown in the previous views, their services being introduced in the late 1870s. There are plenty of cabs available, and several delivery carts in the scene, but the streets were sufficiently safe to allow dogs and children to wander about. At the far end of the square is the century-old Trades Hall which was demolished in 1878 to make way for the Clydesdale Bank building mentioned above.

15 Town House, Dundee
A fine view of the Town House with its 140-feet-high spire; the clock has just struck a quarter-to-four. One of the early electric trams waits to the right; these open-topped vehicles were phased out from 1906 onwards. A conductor from the nearby Tramway offices is standing with a knot of passengers, some of whom were no doubt wishing they had gone by "Kalac cycle" as per the advertisement!

17 Netherkirkgate, Dundee, looking west

A coal cart is stationary on the rough road of the Netherkirkgate; the horse looks in sad need of better feeding. To the right is St Andrew's Roman Catholic Cathedral, a large and impressive building inside with its 1500 seats. Part of the Catholic Church's response to the flood of Irish immigrants—many female—to Dundee in the 1830s and 1840s, it stretched the financial resources of the diocese to the limit, but it was the centre of much culture and charitable work. The fact that the immigrants were nearly all Catholic spared Dundee the sectarian troubles of the west of Scotland; the Orange Order had almost no influence in the City.

18 Whitehall Street, Dundee

Running south from the High Street, Whitehall Street with its legal chambers and elegant shops was laid out in the late 1880s in place of Fish Street as part of the city's drive to clear some of the worst slums. Draffen and Jarvie, later Draffens, remained *in situ* for many decades. The street focuses on the Gilfillan Memorial Church, opened in 1888 (and possessed then of a spire), which honoured the radical U.P. cleric George Gilfillan and which under Donald MacRae offered non-Calvinism and total abstinence to its largely tradesmen membership. It was later to turn to what its own church magazine called a kind of radical Quakerism.

THE ROYAL EXCHANGE, DUNDEE. 2768. G.W.W.

19 Royal Exchange, Dundee

In Panmure Street was situated the Baltic Reading Room, or Merchant's Exchange after its move from the south end of the Wellgate. David Bryce's Flemish design was intended to be capped with a high tower, but settlement of the building during construction in 1855 put a stop to that notion. Next door was to be the Jute Shelter (1882) where the merchants met to set prices for the commodity on which so much of Dundee's economy was based. The statue of James Carmichael still looks across to the Exchange. A crowd of men has gathered to watch the photographer, including two policemen, but not a woman is in sight; all at work, doubtless!

20 Albert Institute, Dundee

Jute merchants stand out in the street as was their preference, rather than work indoors. Behind them is Dundee's memorial to the Prince Consort, acquired by the City in 1879 to continue its usage of museum, picture gallery and library. Queen Victoria had had docks named after her, and a road, but not until her Jubilee in 1897 did the City finally get round to a statue. The figure of Victoria is certainly imperial.

21 Reform Street, Dundee c. 1870

This view, taken from the first floor of the Town House, looks up a street less altered today than most in Dundee. The High School, originally called the Public Seminaries because it combined Dundee's three existing schools, the Academy, the Grammar and the Kirkyard, was built in 1834 after the classical style made popular by the Edinburgh Academy. Just across Euclid Crescent was the General Post Office, open from 6.45 a.m. to 9 p.m. (for the sale of stamps only till 11 p.m.). Nine collections a day were standard. Some sense of the expansion in post office business can be gauged from the statistics of letters handled *each week:* 3,000 in 1838; 90,000 in 1873; 150,000 in 1889!

22 Constitution Road, Dundee

Looking up the hill from the junction of Ward and Meadowside roads, the photograph gives some sense of the steepness of the climb to the north, which must have distressed many a horse. The Dundee and Newtyle Railway originally ran on a parallel course and was forced to use a winding engine to get the carriages up the incline to the Law. To the left is the Baptist Church; the road also included Salem Chapel, the Catholic Apostotlic, Unitarian and Free churches, and one simply called "The Christian Church, ministers various." The YMCA was to have a training school here.

23 Morgan Hospital, Dundee

John Morgan was a Dundee man who made his fortune in India. His bequest of £70,000 was intended to found a high-quality school for the sons of tradesmen and working-class people. Litigation by disappointed relatives was eventually defeated, but one result was that although a fine building was erected for £18,000 in 1863-66, the Trustees found their financial resources so reduced that only 60 of the projected intake of 180 could be admitted. Most of the scholars seem to be gathered here outside for a game of croquet along with three masters and a housekeeper. The hospital became a secondary school after 1872.

BROUGHTY FERRY

In the second half of the nineteenth century Broughty Ferry was expanding rapidly. At one time a small seaport and post-town, with the Castle its only real distinction, its population rose from 2782 in 1851 to 7407 in 1891. Though it was a fishing centre of some significance, employing some 100 boats by the 1890s, what made Broughty Ferry was "its pleasant site, fine air and good sea-bathing" which tempted many of Dundee's mercantile elite to settle there, and drew in large numbers of summer visitors. Prior to the Tay Bridge, Broughty Ferry was the landing point for railway steamers from Newport, and the line from the harbour was heavily used. Its facilities included three bowling clubs, cycling and curling societies and a golf course, eleven churches, several coach-hirers, and an unusual number of teachers. There were no fewer than five Young Ladies Seminaries! McGonagall left this tribute: "The Village of Broughty Ferry is most beautiful to see, with its stately mansions and productive fishing."

24 Broughty Ferry
This fine study of the town is in fact by Valentine, Wilson's great rival. Looking west from the castle, the Edinburgh and Northern (later North British) Railway Company's pier is in the foreground, with a train waiting for the ferry from Fife. A full load is clearly expected as there are no fewer than eight coaches. A few of the town's boats are drawn up on the beach, which is otherwise deserted.

25 Gray Street, Broughty Ferry, c. 1902

Wilson and Co employed a local photographer, Frank Gillies, to take this photograph. He did not have to go far from his Queen Street shop for this view, looking north up Gray Street. Some of the jute barons' houses can be seen on the skyline, but the real fascination lies in the people going unconcernedly about their business. A grandfather and his youngster pause outside Zucconi's Ice Cream Parlour. The Italians dominated this trade everywhere in Scotland: in nearby Dundee there were the Orlandos and the Dunambro family, Montrose was home to the Lazzottis, Forfar to Di Duca Luigi, and so on throughout the East Coast.

.BROUGHTY FERRY LOOKING N. 14,717. G.W.W.

26 Broughty Ferry, looking north

Positioning his camera at the top of the Longlane (St Vincent Place) tenement, the photographer looks north up Gray Street over St Aidan's, past the Broughty Ferry Station. A solitary passenger coach is stationary in front of the U.P. church in Queen Street. Some of the great houses of the Dundee merchant barons can be seen: Craig-gowan, home of James Mudie, steamship owner, Dunalastair, Carbet Castle and Castleroy at the head of the Whinney Brae (Mrs Gilroy). Death duties and dry rot have since taken their toll.

27 Broughty Ferry Castle
The Castle of Burgh Tay, long in ruins, was totally reconstructed by the War Office in 1860-61 at a cost of £7,000. Mounted with some heavy guns, it was manned by a few veterans, and was home to the Tay Volunteer Division of the Royal Engineers, Submarine Miners. The harbour was rebuilt in 1871, and equipped with a stone pier and slip.

28 Beach Crescent, Broughty Ferry
A lemonade cart belonging to Millar & Co of Dundee is doing some trade while the horse gets on with its nose-bag. The promenade is reasonably peopled, with some families and a seaman or two. The third house along on the left is the Orchar Gallery, currently empty, a stone villa built in 1866 for a member of the shipbuilding family of Stephen; the house was gifted to the town by James Orchar Guthrie, Provost of Broughty Ferry, 1886-1888.

MONIFIETH AND CARNOUSTIE

These two communities, like Broughty Ferry, were growing rapidly. Both had large jute works and associated industrial activities and benefitted from their position on the coastal line to the north. Though Monifieth had its attractions for tourists, Carnoustie did particularly well, thanks to its beach and golf course, aided by rigorous promotion from the Railway Companies. The North British Railway Company's official guide, *The Beauties of Scotland,* waxed eloquent:

> "Carnoustie is much favoured as a summer resort, and in regard to golf, invigorating sea-bathing, and pleasant situation, it would be difficult to improve on its seasonable delights."

The Caledonian Railway put Carnoustie second only to St Andrews as a golfing resort, and the town boasted no fewer than four clubs (Caledonia, Carnoustie, Dalhousie and Ladies). The Dalhousie was one of the most expensive in Scotland with an entry fee in 1900 of 105/- (£5.25), and annual subscriptions of 20/- (£1). It still had 390 members, as against the 260 of the cheaper Caledonia, whose entry fee was only 20/- (£1) with an annual subscription of 10/- 6d (52.5p). There was even a golf instructor, John Fox, for the benefit of those wishing to improve their game. Carnoustie also benefitted from the establishment in 1895 of the Army firing ranges and training area on Barry Links, long a favourite camping ground for volunteer and regular soldiers alike.

29 At the tee, Monifieth, c. 1905
The popularity of golf amongst all sections of the community is evident from this queue of golfers waiting to go off at the first tee. The clientele here appear mostly to be artisan, and while there are some boys, no caddies are to be seen. The men of Monifieth carried their own clubs. Behind the player about to drive is a long board with balls lodged in order of arrival, the traditional way of booking your turn at the tee. It would be interesting to know how many were using clubs made locally in Monifieth, either by James Smith of Princes Street or James Watson of Dalhousie Street

30 Carnoustie, at the beach

A summer scene with the beach well tenanted. Some are at work on sandcastles, others wait for a pony ride, and in the centre a children's meeting appears to be in progress. Several seaside communities supported Beach Missions, with choruses and competitions. Three bathing machines stand near the high-water mark; these probably belonged to the enterprising John Robb who also handled the rental of apartments to visitors. What strikes one is how well-dressed everyone is, and the array of umbrellas or parasols.

31 Carnoustie, from the golf course

The links at Carnoustie supported both a full 18-hole men's course, and a much shorter ladies' course. Ladies were excluded from the main course, it being considered by male authority that they could only manage holes seventy or eighty yards long, with an occasional obstruction. Things have changed since! The burn is a principal hazard still, though more channelled. Charles Brand's workshop is visible to the left; he was still advertising himself as a maker of golf-balls as well as clubs in the early 1900s. The Caledonian (1887) and the Dalhousie Clubhouses are there yet.

32 Sunday afternoon concert on Carnoustie Links, c. 1900

Part of the seaside experience was to listen to the band. Quite a good crowd is gathered for this Sunday afternoon concert, even if some of the children are totally uninterested. The band may well have been from the local Panmure Works, a big jute and linen firm.

ARBROATH

Arbroath was the second largest town in Angus, with a population of 22,987 in 1891, double what it had been in 1851 at 10,030. It was a centre of textile manufacture with over 30 spinning mills and works, its speciality being sailcloth, canvas and coarse linen. Firms such as David Corsar & Sons (Nursery and Almerieclose mills), Andrew Lowson Ltd. (Green's mills, Baltic works) and Frances Webster & Sons (Alma works) were internationally famous. But Arbroath was not a one-horse town. Its economy was much more diversified than Dundee's and its fishing, tanneries and boot and shoe works provided work for men as well as women, something on which *The Arbroath Guide* commented in its leader of September 30th, 1905:

"It is largely women whose work produces the great individual fortunes . . . and on whom the whole prosperity of Dundee is founded. But for the cheap labour of its women, Dundee from being an important city would shrivel up to the dimensions of a small town. In Arbroath it has been gratifying to see that new industrial enterprise has been of a character as to lead to the employment of men."

Apart from the Abbey, the town of Arbroath offered the tourist relatively little, lacking as it did a sandy beach although it did have excellent parks and pleasure grounds, cliffs and caves. It was a good centre for walks and excursions to nearby St Vigeans or Auchmithie. Local hotels offered coaching tours to Lunan Bay on which much hope was pinned. The North British Railway guide thought the sands magnificent and regretted they were not situated within "closer hail of some great populous centre." The Bell Rock lighthouse was constantly visited by boatmen.

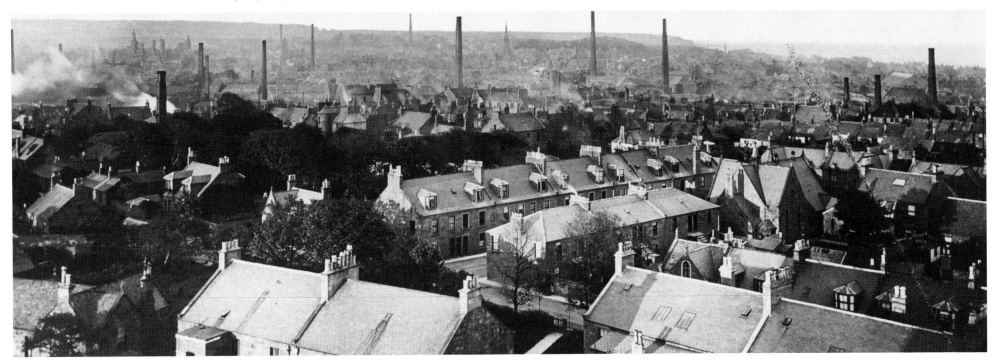

33 Arbroath from the Water Tower

This popular vantage point to the west of the station at Nolt Loan was much loved by Victorian photographers, though the view nowadays is obscured by the trees which have grown up round the Tower. The houses in Addison Place are still there, but most of the factory "lums" are gone, as is Duke Street Church which was demolished in the 1980s. The water tower was completed in 1885 at a cost of £7000. Arbroath Public Library has a photograph of the workforce employed on this project, with biographical details. Archibald Anderson, the mason carpenter, went out to the United States shortly after the work was completed and never returned. Every issue of the *Arbroath Herald* carried advertisements by emigration agencies.

34 Arbroath from Cairnie Hill

Judging from the absence of smoke, production seems to have been suspended at all the town mills. The ''Round O'' of the Abbey is clearly visible, whereas the many mills and fish curing works must normally have made Arbroath a smokey town indeed! The large canvas and sailcloth Dens Works borders the railway on the east, again apparently not working, and the absence of carriages in the engine-shed sidings—there is a string of Caledonian Railway coal-wagons—suggests that this is a public holiday, perhaps the St Thomas holiday so much beloved by the citizens. Arbroath was a very active centre of the earliest railways in Scotland in the late 1830s, with the fifteen-mile line to Forfar completed in January 1839, and a line of similar length to Dundee later that same year.

35 Old Shorehead, Arbroath

Otherwise known as Danger Point, Shorehead was the place at which the Brothock Burn reached the sea. The burn had been horribly polluted, acting as it did as a receptacle for all the town's sewage, but in 1872 a main drain was put in to divert the worst impurities away—to general relief, no doubt. George Hay (*Aberbrothick Illustrated,* 1886) speaks of one of the commonest sights here being ''that of fisher wives and girls washing fishy clothes in the burn.'' In this view there are clothes out to dry, both on the bridge (now widened) and on the drying line in front of Oldshorehead House. A boy wheels a barrow with canvas whilst a coachman waits in the background.

36 Protection wall, Arbroath

The tide is full in against the harbour wall, on the top of which the photographer has perched his camera. The shipyard is empty, as it was from 1881 onwards for many years, but Arbroath boats are tied up all round the harbour. In 1891 the fishing employed 146 boats, with over 600 men and boys. Some boat names are partially visible: *Beth and Three Sisters, Helen Smith.* In the foreground sails are spread out for patching, while a horse waits with a load of stone to renew the inner face of the harbour. The harbour trustees found their financial task a heavy one, with not enough revenue even to service the debt incurred in rebuilding the harbour in the 1870s. Eventually the Government intervened to halve the amount owed.

37 High Street, Arbroath

The lamp on the left outside the Sheriff Court House is still there, as is the watchmaker, Willocks, on the right, though the Clydesdale Bank has had a third storey added. The Temperance Society established in 1837 and supposed at one time to have had 1500 members had an uphill struggle in Arbroath with its 80 grocers and spirit dealers. The High Street has several bars, the Thistle, Oriental, Shakespeare and Doig's (centre of picture), plus the White Hart and Royal Hotels. The cart on the right is clearly carrying something liquid—milk perhaps?

ARBROATH ABBEY. WEST DOOR. 932. G.W.W.

38 Arbroath Abbey, west door

All tourists made their way here to the picturesque, if chaotic, ruins of the Abbey founded in 1178 by William I and dedicated to St Thomas a-Becket. After the Reformation it fell on hard times, and much stone was robbed for other town buildings. Eventually the Barons of the Scottish Exchequer stepped in to undertake some remedial work in 1815, rebuilding the circular window. Tidying up was much needed, but at least the west door was reasonably intact. A boy sits inside the arch: a typical GWW touch.

39 Arbroath Abbey, west door

Graffiti is no new problem! Andrew Sikkies is immortalised in this photograph. That this was no isolated episode is proven by a leader in the *Arbroath Guide* on the occasion of the installation of new seats on the Common, hoping that they would "not be defaced by the pen-knives of lads ambitious of seeing their initials carved in permanent places . . ."

(August 20th, 1870).

41 Victoria Park, Arbroath c. 1897
Arbroath marked Victoria's Jubilee by the opening of a new park, purchased from a local landowner by public subscription. On opening day, June 26th, there was a great procession through the town to the park where sports were held. These included a "character race," greasy pole, tug of war, and a ladies' cycle race. The Volunteers were there, and as this photograph shows, the attendance was huge: the *Arbroath Herald* said that "not far short of 20,000 of the inhabitants of Arbroath must have turned out."

40 Arbroath Abbey, ancient tomb
The sad thing about this ornate 1674 tomb is how badly it has weathered since GWW took this photograph, which we can date to some time between 1869 and 1886, thanks to William Straton and his family whose headstone is to the right. Anna (d. 1869) is the last name, but to come was William, in January 1886. Tombs fascinated the Victorians, and some of the finest early Scottish photography took place in churchyards.

MONTROSE

In 1901 the Caledonian Railway waxed lyrical about the attractions of Montrose: ''a favourite watering place and health resort, with its four miles of magnificent sandy beach, its capital golf links and its unsurpassed facilities for rowing, cycling, cricket and other sports.'' It was as well for Montrose that tourism *was* on the increase, because otherwise the economy of the town was faltering in the later nineteenth century. True, the flax spinning works still employed large numbers, fishing and fish-curing were doing well, and the long-established firm of Robert Millar & Sons controlled an enormous trade in dressed timber, believed to be second in scale only to Greenock. But the town's emigration agencies found plenty of interest in times of depression, and Montrose's population had fallen from 15,239 in 1851 to 13,098 in 1891. The flood of summer visitors was, therefore, most welcome to the town's hoteliers, shopkeepers, stablers and booksellers.

42 Montrose Beach
The sands of Montrose were a major attraction for families, and a few hardy souls can be seen on what clearly is a breezy day. Two ladies shelter in the lee of the boatshed, but others are about to swim as the horseman waits to take the elegant bathing machines to the water's edge. A swing sways in the wind while in front, a young man halts to have his picture taken. How elegant his dress is, with cane, stiff collar and black tie!

43 Montrose Golf Course

Montrose links were reckoned to be amongst the best golf courses in Scotland and the town's advertising constantly played on the attractions of the course. The "eminent golfing authority," Mr Horace Hutchison, called it one of the best three in Scotland. Of large extent, 3¼ miles, the course was kept in good order. "Capitally laid out, the well devised hazards add to the interest of the game." There was a minimal charge to visitors—5/- (25p) a month—and despite the presence of several golf clubs, the course was never overcrowded. There was a Ladies' Course, much shorter in length, but still 18 holes, with 150 members in 1900 paying a mere 2/- 6d (12.5p) per annum in subscriptions. Here a solitary lady takes a posed and unenthusiastic stance for the photographer. Perhaps she had been persuaded away from the Ladies' clubhouse just behind. Also visible is the much more substantial clubhouse of the Royal Albert G.C. (captain, in 1900, the honorable C. M. Ramsay), with 125 members and an annual subscription of 21/- (105p). The town had two makers of golf clubs; J&W Craigie and James Linton, both with premises nearby.

44 Paton's Factory, Montrose

This long-established firm dating from 1795 employed in the late nineteenth century about a thousand workers, two-thirds of whom were female. In front of their 1828 building—still standing but now in different hands—are the newly laid-out Mid-links Gardens, the chief features of which were the two large circular flower and shrub beds, one with statue. Behind the nymph is a large and expensive lamp, presented by one Scott, Dean of Guild in 1881, known simply as "The Dean's Lamp." Not far away was the town band-stand where concerts were regularly performed.

45 Ferry Den, Montrose
Ferryden used to be the place where travellers from the south took the ferry for Montrose, and long after the Inch bridge was built across to Rossie Island, the ferryboat continued to ply its trade: the 300 yard sail cost all of one halfpenny in 1881! Ferryden's prosperity was based on its fishing, and prosperous indeed were the Ferryden men, owners of their boats and their houses alike, besides large deposits in the Savings Banks. Several smartly-painted boats with their Montrose registration are to be seen, including the *Peggy,* ME 583. A woman is gutting a last box of fish.

46 Distant View of Montrose
Visitors to Montrose were strongly recommended to take the ferry to Ferryden and then walk up to the Craig Braes which offered this superb vantage point. Inchbrayock Island, with its burial ground then still in use, lies in the middle of the South Esk estuary. Beyond, the steeple of the Old Parish Church dominates the skyline of Montrose.

MONTROSE SUSPENSION BRIDGE. 13,622. G.W.W.

47 Montrose Suspension Bridge
A man and his curly-coated retriever pose in front of the suspension bridge carrying the main road south. Built in 1829 and taken down a hundred years later, the bridge tended to sway in the wind by as much as 3 or 4 feet. In 1840 a boating regatta attracted large crowds of spectators to the bridge and as the boats passed underneath, the people rushed to the other side. One of the chains gave way and six spectators were killed. The bridge was subsequently strengthened. The track of the Wharf Street branch railway can be seen and, on the opposite hill, Craig Church.

48 Montrose Steeple

The new steeple of the Old Parish Church erected in 1832-34 rises 220 feet high. Not surprisingly, it is hard to find anywhere in Montrose from which it is not visible! The church was (and is) one of the largest in Scotland, with 2500 seats, and at the time of this photograph had recently acquired a fine organ. Business appears slack on a fine summer's afternoon, the windows are wide open for air, but the shop blinds are hard down. Balfour the bookseller was a familiar feature of the High Street for many years.

49 High Street Montrose

From the grubbiness of the Central Hotel built in 1894 (to left), this view must have been taken some years after its opening. Joseph Hume's statue surveys the Town House from which this view is taken. Born in Montrose and long MP for the burgh, the statue by Calder Marshall was unveiled in 1859. Notice the walkways across the road; pavements had only recently been laid in the town.

50 Melville Gardens, Montrose

The town did much to enhance its facilities for residents and visitors alike, and these Gardens with their tennis courts, croquet and bowling greens were reclaimed from the waste lands of the mid-links in the early 1880s. To the right is the magnificent terrace of Melville Garden's Victoria Villas built in 1887, and then largely occupied by retired people.

Murray's *Handbook* was not enthusiastic about Forfar. "Bristling with chimneys, it is by no means an attractive town." But it was a thriving textile town, with at the turn of the century no fewer than eight factories and two bleach works employing over 3000 hands. Its public facilities were impressive: libraries, institutes, halls and parks, and as elsewhere a remarkable range of societies and clubs including: a choral union, YMCA, golf, angling, bowling and football clubs, and two strong masonic lodges. Forfar was also a major market and railway centre. Visitors came to the burgh to the Loch, or the site of Forfar Castle: the Witches' Howe and the Forfar Bridle. Like Montrose, but not to the same extent, it was losing population, from 13,579 in 1881 to 12,769 ten years later.

FORFAR FROM BALMASHANNER HILL. 13,839. G.W.W.

51 Forfar from Balmashanner Hill
"There are few finer scenes than meets the gaze from Balmashanner's brow," so wrote the local historian Alan Reid in 1902, and you can see why the photographer made his way to this observation spot. The town and its mills lie below, the Grampians to the north. Glen Clova and Glen Esk were very popular with tourist excursions. To the left, beyond the Congregational Manse, is the Reid Park donated to the town by ex-Provost Peter Reid in 1896. The sixteen-acre park, with its bandstand and walks, was opened by the eminent politician, John Morley, in June of that year.

52 Reid Hall, Forfar

Another of Peter Reid's benefactions to his native town was the Reid Hall. Work started in August 1869 and took several years to complete, costing Reid over £10,000. The basis of Reid's fortune was his business as a confectioner, his speciality being Forfar Rock. Over the years his gifts totalled over £25,000, no mean sum, and it was only right that a statue of Reid was later commissioned by the community. The hall was run by Reid himself for many years, but then handed over to the Town Council. It was for public meetings and entertainment. A poster advertises the forthcoming visit on 30th September 1905 of the Royal Imperial Pictures Company, with an exhibition of animated pictures, plus a magnificent reproduction of the Royal Review of Scottish Volunteers. The hall must have been filled to capacity, as the *Forfar Herald* reported that there was a "Capital company."

53 Castle Street, Forfar

Looking south to the Municipal Buildings, opened in 1871, formerly the County buildings and used by the Sheriff Court. The Town Council held regular monthly meetings there, and various officials had their quarters there including the gas manager. William Urquhart's tea bazaar at number 57 carries a board stating modestly "For Purity, Strength, Fragrance, Our Teas are Superb!" Several panniers of crockery carefully packed in straw have just arrived at James Shepherd's China Shop two doors up, and on the other side of the road, a bolt of cloth rests on top of a case outside the Forfar Hat & Cap Shop. Forfar had once been the centre of a manufacture of wooden-soled shoes or clogs, but the "sutors" craft was much reduced by the late nineteenth century.

54 Castle Street, Forfar, looking north

Looking the opposite way from the previous photograph, there are several interesting differences. The public urinal outside the Town house is still there, as is Urquhart's tea shop, though his sign now reads "Drink Urquhart's Famed Teas." In the centre of the street is Peter Reid's statue in bronze, sitting rather than standing or riding which tended to be the general custom in Victorian times. The granite pedestal provided a useful lounging perch for those not at work. Reid's statue was unveiled on Saturday, 3rd February, 1899: "the crowd cheered to echo the well-known features so skillfully portrayed by the artist, and the Instrumental Band struck up 'A Man's a Man for a' that' amidst a scene of the greatest enthusiasm."

55 East High Street, Forfar, from East Port
This end of the High Street towards the Arbroath Road was well supplied with licensed premises. Forfar had 27 public houses in 1900, whose trade must have been heaviest on Mondays when the weekly cattle market was held. Here can be seen three, the Forfar Arms (Allsopps Ales), the Balmoral Inn (Wines and Spirits) and the Volunteer Arms— temperance work was an uphill task in Forfar!.

56 East High Street, Forfar, looking west

A gloomy day with not much happening even in the town's main thoroughfare. The Episcopal Church to the right, erected 1879-81, still lacks its projected spire. A mere 40 feet of the intended 163 were completed before the money ran out. No such problem affected the parish church whose 150-foot spire retained pole position. Just in front of it are the premises of one of the town's photographers, David Laing. Nearby was the enterprising chemist, J. A. MacRossen, who sold photographic materials, cameras, plates, paper and materials. His special product was a perfume called the Strathmore Bouquet, "a compound of the indescribable odours of spring."

57 The Pend, Forfar

Just off East High Street lies the Pend, to which Osnaburg and other linens were brought in the early nineteenth century to be inspected by an official of the Board of Trustees. If acceptable, the clothes were stamped with his name so that if the buyer were dissatisfied, he could bring an action against the official rather than the weaver, which encouraged the stampmaster to do his job properly. The system was abolished in 1823 but the name stuck. The principle of personal liability for public work might be worth reviving!

Six miles west-north-west of Forfar, on a Caledonian Railway branch line, lay Kirriemuir. It had long been a brisk little manufacturing town with a particular trade in brown linen; in good years around the turn of the century, output ran as high as 100,000 pieces, varying in length from 100 to 170 yards, and 1500 of the town's population of 3800 in 1891 were employed in that industry. J. M. Barrie put Kirriemuir on the map, transforming a quiet little upland town, known to some as a holiday haunt and health resort, into ''a place of pilgrimage.'' Kirriemuir was a centre for excursions; coaches went daily to Glen Prosen and Kirkton of Clova. In the vicinity were several castles in various states of repair: Inverquharity, Airlie, Cortachy and Glamis.

58 Kirriemuir from the Cemetery
A windless summer's day allows the camera to catch the Kirriemuir panorama from the cemetery to the north. The smoke belches straight up from one of the Bellie's Brae linen works, and the Old Parish Church clock hands proclaim the time to be twenty-minutes-to-noon. Not far from where this view was taken at the top of cemetery, Barrie was to be buried in 1937 after a funeral service in the local St Mary's Episcopal Church, chosen in preference to Westminster Abbey.

59 Handloom weaver at work

Once, handloom weaving had been the most prosperous of artisan crafts in Scotland. A hundred years previously every other male in Kirriemuir would have had his loom. But thanks to the power loom, the weaving had fallen on hard times, and by the 1890s there were few left. To scrape a living, the weaver would have had to work a long day, six days a week. The loom was bedded into the earth for stability, but even with that cushioning the thump of the loom used quickly to loosen the roof slates.

60 An old handloom weaver at T'nowhead

One group whom J. M. Barrie captured well in his novels of "Thrums" were the Auld Lichts, the stern hell-fire Presbyterians of the Original Secession Church whose Sabbath began on Saturday evening at six when all weaving ceased. Their permitted reading was the Bible or *Pilgrim's Progress*. Knowhead or T'nowhead Farm lay on the Blairgowrie road just to the west of town, and presumably this patriach was mulling over the morning sermon in the Auld Licht Kirk. Barrie's followers would have associated T'nowhead with a rather different episode: the Sabbath-breaking race of weaver Sam and carter Saunders for T'nowhead's Bell.

61 "A window in Thrums"

Just across the road lay another place made famous by Barrie, the cottage home of Hendry McQumpha, at whose window the housebound Jess sat for 20 years. Is the lad meant to remind us of her Joey, killed by a cart? Notice the advertisement offering "Souvenirs of Thrums, Lemonade and Biscuits": visitors could also get Thrums boots, Thrums pies, even a Thrums blend of old Scotch whisky!

62 High Street and Town House, Kirriemuir

The Town Hall—to right with clock—was the oldest building in Kirriemuir and had been the Tolbooth. It later became the Stampmaster's Office, and later still it had become the Post Office, the business being run by one David Buchanan who managed to combine the roles of chemist, druggist, postman and insurance agent. Kirriemuir had a wide range of shops including a Cycle store and a Taxidermist ("Stags heads always in stock") and several tailors offering stalking suits, shooting, fishing and golfing capes, cycling outfits, riding habits and travelling wraps. Here the shops include W. B. Mills, who published the *Kirriemuir Advertiser* every Friday, Milne the hatter, Adam George, boot and shoe manufacturer, and at number 27, David Leslie, a grocer. He sent out a van to nearby localities and promised visitors to this "salubrious and bracing countryside" that he kept a large stock of well selected goods. One o'clock it is by the Church clock though the Town House lags a few minutes behind, but nothing much appears to be happening to disturb the spaniel seated in the middle of the square!

THE BIRTHPLACE OF J.M.BARRIE, KIRRIEMUIR. 11849. G.W.W.

63 Barrie's birthplace, Kirriemuir

James Barrie was born at 9 Brechin Road in 1860. His father, a handloom weaver, worked downstairs while the family lived upstairs. The whole street was a weaving colony, and on most days the clack of the looms must have been continuous. This side of the tenements was said to have been better behaved than the other, because it lay within sight of the Auld Licht Manse. The enterprising David Young of Thrums Palace, a fruit shop, offered visitors two celebrated rocks in packets, 3d and 6d (1.25p and 2.5p) each, in wrappers bearing a true picture of the Window in Thrums and Barrie's birthplace.

BRECHIN

Brechin was doing well in the late nineteenth century. *Murray's Handbook* (1903) describes it as a flourishing town, with its linen works, paperworks and distilleries. Certainly it was prosperous enough to support a servant's register (the Misses Mitchell, High Street), a wide range of shops and services, and an extraordinary range of societies such as the Horticultural, Book and Tract, Literary and Mutual Improvement. Clubs for bowling, cricket, curling, football and golf were well-supported, as were temperance societies. Brechin had no fewer than five, including the "Pride of Esk" and the "Hope of Angus." Music-making was a feature of Brechin's life, with a City Band, Pipe Band, two Quadrille Bands and the Ramsay Brass Band. But Brechin, like the other towns of Angus, had times of depression, and each issue of the annual *Brechin Almanack* carried advertisements from shipping companies and emigration agents. The best-known of these were Black & Johnston in the High Street, who combined printing, bookselling, dealing in music and instruments ("pianofortes, American organs and harmoniums") with their role as licensed emigration agents. At least Brechin managed to hold its population pretty steady between 1881 and 1901 at around 10,500. For the tourist, there was much to see in the vicinity and in Brechin itself, the Round Tower of the Cathedral being a particular draw. Excursions set off each day in the summer to Loch Lee, Banchory, Ballater, Edzell, Glenesk and elsewhere. Some of the tours were run from local hotels, of which Brechin had a number which were reckoned to be of very good quality, but Greig's Posting Establishment would hire out carriages, brakes and waggonettes; the Panmure Stables hired out horses and drivers ("careful and experienced only") if desired.

64 Brechin Station

The Caledonian Station at Brechin was and is a most elegant terminus. The railway first reached Brechin in 1846, but the whole station had to be considerably enlarged with the opening of the Forfar and Brechin line in 1895 and the branch to Edzell in the following year. Eight trains a day, the six-mile journey took 19 minutes. Coal waggons are being off-loaded to the left, and some barrels await collection by the Glencadam distillery. The track work shows how much traffic the station handled, both passenger and freight.

65 Brechin from the south

This panorama, taken sometime in the 1880s, sweeps round from the Andover Tower of the Tenements' School on the right, past the linen mills and paper works to Brechin Castle and the Cathedral on the left. The Tenements' School was paid for by three Brechinites who had made good in America. Chief amongst these was John Smith of Andover in Massachusetts. In the foreground is the south lodge of Brechin Castle, with washing hanging out in the garden

66 Brechin from the Bridge

Looking along the South Esk from the Bridge towards the paper mills, River Street is neatly laid out as an esplanade. Thanks to a legacy from a former rector of the Grammar School, River Street had been tidied up in 1879-80 with the demolition of some old hovels at the waterside. A protection wall was built, and a donation from ex-Provost Duncan provided the iron railings. Behind the Rob Roy tavern (then James Fearn's, later Peter Pollock's) rises the Maison Dieu United Free Church in Witchden Road, opened in April 1892.

67 The Mechanics' Institute, Brechin

Now over one hundred and fifty years old, the Mechanics' Institute, or to give its full title, the Mechanics' Literary and Scientific Institute, was gifted by Lord Panmure in 1838, the foundation stone being laid on the 28th June, Queen Victoria's Coronation Day. The architect was a local man, John Henderson, born at the Den Nursery, who established quite a national reputation; his other work including extensions at Glenalmond College. Membership of the Institute which cost 2/- (10p) a year to tradesmen and journeymen—3/- (15p) to other people—in the late nineteenth century gave access to an excellent library, reading rooms and billiard club. The imposing fountain in front was erected in 1877 by Lady Christian Maule in memory of her brother, the last Baron Panmure. It was removed to St Ninian's Square by the Council in 1895.

68 Church Street, Brechin

At the junction of High Street and Church Street, a delivery boy pauses with a tray of "softies" from Alexander Belford's shop. Belford's offered everything from infants' rusks to Madeira cakes. Another branch of the business in Market Street was sole agent for the Salvation Army teas. Next to Belford's is the town house built in 1788, complete with bell and clock, and used until 1895 when the council removed to new Municipal Buildings in Bank Street. Across the road (and was that just a coincidence?) is the Alma Inn and Hotel, later renamed the Bolag. A delivery dray is at the door. In the distance is the tower of the Mechanics' Institute.

69 High Street, Brechin
If the Town House clock is to be believed, this photograph was taken nearly an hour before the previous view of Church Street. A policeman stands outside and various adults, children and dogs appear to be more interested in the photographer than anything else. A number of trade signs are visible above the shops; a large riding boot for Ramsay Kidd's Shoemaking business, a chemist's mortar and pestle, and the snuff-taking Highlander of the tobacconist, John Oswald.

70 St David Street, Brechin
A crocodile of schoolchildren carrying their books tied in bundles make their way home. One has her name on a hairband—was Jane Nelson very forgetful or her mother over-protective? Even in the nineteenth century the roads were always being dug up. This time it was for the installation of electric cables by the Angus Electric Light and Power Company, the supply being turned on in 1901. Most of the factories had had their own generators since the early 1890s. A gas street lamp is in the process of conversion at the High Street junction opposite the Dalhousie Hotel.

71 St Ninian's Square, Brechin

St Ninian's Square was made into a neat garden in the mid-1890s when the Dalhousie Memorial was moved there. Behind it is Bank Street United Presbyterian Church, built in 1873-4, but the real feature of the Square is the public library. No self-respecting Victorian community could be without one, but despite a generous bequest, it took time to persuade Brechin's ratepayers to dig into their pockets. The foundation stone was laid with full masonic honours—how things are changed today—on the 5th December 1891, and the Library opened in July 1893. On average, 3000 volumes were borrowed each month, which suggests a high level of usage in Brechin, given the existence of the Institute Library as well.

72 Maulesden, near Brechin

Just to the west of Brechin beyond the Castle lay Maulesden, built in 1853 to a Bryce design for the Honorable William Maule. After his death, it passed into the possession of one of the Cox textile dynasty from Dundee who spent much time and money on improving the grounds. In 1892 it was bought by a prosperous linen manufacturer from Forfar, J. B. Don. This house, like so many others in Angus, has since gone, demolished in 1963 to join such other mansions as Aldbar (burnt down in 1964) and Panmure (blown up in 1955). Here, on a pleasant spring day, the servants are taking advantage of the weather to air the linen with sheets hanging out of most windows.

73 The Den, Brechin

The town did have a public park, opened in 1867, and the Trinity Muir with its golf course, but a favourite walk for the older generation was through the Den, "the Bonnie Braes" part of which was Henderson's Nursery. Shrubs and young trees are lined out in orderly rows; some of these no doubt would find their way to the mansions and villas in and around Brechin. A substantial bridge carries the road across to the Town Cemetery, the new lodge to which can be seen on the right, it was built in 1876 when the cemetery was enlarged. At the junction of Panmure and Southesk Streets is the East United Free Church, with its massive steeple. The religious census of 12th December 1881 showed 368 worshippers there; that of March 31st 1901 found only 315. Brechin as a whole still had a very respectable rate of attendance—2127 out of 10,444—but the Church was steadily losing ground even before the First World War. The most famous of Brechin's many ministers was the Reverend James McCosh, later first President of Princeton University in the USA where he arranged bursaries for Brechin's young men.

74 Kinnaird Castle

The most sumptuous mansion in Angus, according to the *Cambridge County Georgraphy* of 1912. Kinnaird was a very large castle indeed, with 30 bedrooms and nine public rooms, to say nothing of library, conservatory, kitchens and servants' quarters. The sixth Earl of Southesk had Kinnaird rebuilt in the late 1850s to a design by Bryce, but unlike Maulesden the style chosen was that of a French chateau. It is an imposing pile, the product of an age when servants were readily available.

75 Glamis Castle

One of the most popular tourist attractions in Scotland, thanks to Sir Walter Scott's publicising of the secret chamber in his *Letters on Demonology and Witchcraft*—and of course to Shakespeare's *Macbeth*.

EDZELL & LOCHLEE

Edzell was reckoned a neat little village, "suitable for staying at" (*Murray's Handbook*) with its good hotels, the Panmure and the Glenesk. While Edzell had long attracted visitors for fishing and shooting, it was the coming of the railway that opened up the area to large numbers of summer sightseers. One of the last lines to be built in Scotland, the ceremonial cutting of the first sod of the Brechin and Edzell Railway was performed by Mrs Shaw Anderson of Coveston on June 2nd, 1894. The short 6-mile branch was opened in 1896 and did help to bring trade to the town but, thanks to the motor car, lorry and bus, it was never profitable. Passenger services to Edzell were withdrawn in 1931, though the line hung on for freight until 1964. Edzell Castle was a popular destination for excursionists.

76 Edzell Golf Course

The golf course at Edzell was an attraction for visitors. Special cheap tickets were available from the railways to members of golf clubs elsewhere in Scotland wishing to play at Edzell. The station is behind the course with a set of carriages waiting at the platform while the engine takes on water. A gentleman is about to drive to the last hole, a left-hander apparently. It is a little curious why he is playing from beside the tee, rather than on it. It looks as if caddies were in short supply locally since it appears that his daughter, under the enormous cap, has been pressed into service

77 Panmure Arms Hotel, Edzell

Both of Edzell's principal hotels had to be enlarged in the late nineteenth century to cope with the surge of tourists. The Glenesk added a new wing, but the Panmure was to be transformed almost out of recognition, becoming a four-storey pile in mock-Tudor style. Here in this damaged photograph a groom holds his horse while the rider leans against the railings, and a touring party is about to depart—for Fettercairn or Tayside perhaps? The hotel had access to fishing and shooting for guests, plus a well-appointed billiards room.

78 Dalhousie Arch, Edzell

This arch in memory of the 13th Earl of Dalhousie and his wife Ida was erected in 1888 by their tenants, shocked at their early deaths at 40 and 30 respectively, within a day of each other in November 1887. Two lady cyclists are en route to Brechin, while through the Arch can be seen the Inglis Memorial Hall, opened in 1898. To the left is the Glenesk Hotel; a shilling (5p) a day for bed and attendance in 1903.

79 Church Street, Edzell
Running parallel with the High Street was Church Street; the Parish church is at the far end. Edzell was much admired as a village full of neat stone houses, with flower plots in front and back gardens for vegetables. The village had its own gas works and the streets were well-lit, even if the roads and pavements must have been muddy in anything other than dry weather. Hence the boot scrapers outside each door!

80 Lochlee, Glenesk
A favourite destination for visitors was the old churchyard at the east end of Lochlee. Queen Victoria and Albert went there in September 1861, ''a wild but not large lake,'' she called Lochlee in her *Leaves from the Journal of our Life in the Highlands*. The widowed Victoria was to return four years later. Coach tours ran to Lochlee from Edzell and Brechin. The Crown Hotel at Brechin ran a special four-in-hand coach ''Olden Times,'' three days a week; fare 3/- 6d (17.5p), return 5s (25p), box seat 1/- (5p) extra. It must have been a long day.